Boats

Daphne Butler

623.82 (B)

SIMON & SCHUSTER

LONDON • SYDNEY • NEW YORK • TOKYO • SINGAPORE • TORONTO

S310810

Notes for parents and teachers

This book has a theme that threads its way through the topic. It does not aim to deal with the topic comprehensively; rather it aims to provoke thought and discussion. Each page heading makes a simple statement about the illustration which is then amplified and questioned by the text. Material in this book is particularly relevant to the following sections of the National Curriculum:

English: AT2 levels 1–3
Science: AT1 levels 1–2, AT10 levels 1–3

 Remember to warn children that water is never ever safe.

TAKE ONE has been researched and compiled by Simon & Schuster Young Books. We are very grateful for the support and guidance provided by our advisory panel of professional educationalists in the course of the production.

Advisory panel:
Colin Pidgeon, Headteacher
Wheatfields Junior School, St Albans
Deirdre Walker, Deputy headteacher
Wheatfields Junior School, St Albans
Judith Clarke, Headteacher
Grove Infants School, Harpenden

British Library Cataloguing in Publication Data
Butler, Daphne, 1945–
  Boats.
  1. Boats
  I. Title II. Series
  623.82

ISBN 0–7500–0288–3

Series editor: Daphne Butler
Design: M&M Design Partnership
Photographs: ZEFA

First published in Great Britain in 1990
by Simon & Schuster Young Books

Simon & Schuster Young Books
Simon & Schuster Ltd
Wolsey House, Wolsey Road
Hemel Hempstead, Herts HP2 4SS

© 1990 Simon & Schuster Young Books

Printed and bound in Great Britain
by BPCC Paulton Books Ltd

Contents

Over the rocks   6–7

Wide and slow   8–9

Boats with engines   10–11

At the sea   12–13

Take a ferry   14–15

At the port   16–17

How much cargo?   18–19

Tug boats   20–21

Passenger boats   22–23

On the bridge   24–25

Out to sea   26–27

Before engines   28–29

Index   30–31

Over the rocks

The river is rushing down the
mountain over the rocks.
Canoes and rafts float on the water
and are steered past the rocks.

Look at the shapes of the boats.
Why do you think they float?

7

Wide and slow

The river is moving slowly across
the flat land.   This is a safer
place for rowing or learning to sail.

What makes these boats move
through the water?

Boats with engines

Barges carry goods on the river.
The goods are called cargo.
Other boats carry passengers.

These boats are big and heavy, and
have engines to drive them
through the water.

ВАСИЛИЙ СУРИКОВ
МОСКВА

11

At the sea

The river has reached the sea.
Fishing boats are tied up along
the banks of the river.

The boats go out to sea to catch fish.
Nets are dragged behind them in
the water.

13

Take a ferry

Ferry boats carry cars, lorries and people.
The cars and lorries are carefully loaded.

This is a heavy boat.
Why do you think it floats?

At the port

Huge boats are loaded with cargo.
It is packed into boxes called containers.

Can you see the containers on the deck?
The boat must be very heavy.

Does all cargo travel in containers?

17

JERVIS BAY

LONDON

KEEP CLEAR OF PROPELLER

40
39 12M
38   8
37   4
36 11M
35   8
34   4
33 10M
32   8

18

How much cargo?

This boat is empty so it is floating high in the water.   When it is loaded with cargo, it sinks down.

Can you see the numbers on the back of the boat?   The water comes up to these numbers when the boat is loaded with cargo.

Tug boats

Some cargo boats are huge and cannot move easily inside the port.

They need small boats called tugs to tow them in and out.

BRITISH RESOLUTION
LONDON

21

22

Passenger boats

Once, people sailed round the world
in big boats called passenger liners.
It took 6 weeks to sail from
Europe to Australia.

How do most people go to and from
Australia today?

On the bridge

The Captain steers the boat from
a room called the bridge.   He has
many instruments to help him.

A large boat takes a long time
to slow down or turn.
Why do you think this is?

Out to sea

The Captain must look out for
dangers at sea.   He must not
hit rocks or other boats.
Remember a big boat turns slowly.

Can you think of other dangers?

Before engines

Large boats need engines to drive
them through the water.   The bigger
the boat, the more powerful
the engine needs to be.

How did boats move through the
water before engines were invented?

Index

barges 10

bridge 24

canoes 6

Captain 24, 27

cargo 10, 16, 19

cargo boats 20

containers 16

dangers 27

deck 16

engines 10, 29

ferry boats 15